THE POETRY OF SCOTLAND

'Winter Gleam, Angus'. *James McIntosh Patrick*

THE POETRY OF
SCOTLAND

Edited by
Douglas Dunn

B. T. BATSFORD LTD LONDON

ATHOL BROSE

Charm'd with a drink which Highlanders compose,
  A German traveller exclaim'd with glee, –
'Potztausend! sare, if dis is Athol Brose,
  How goot dere Athol Boetry must be!'

Thomas Hood (1799–1845)

First published 1979
Copyright selection Douglas Dunn 1979
Set in Monophoto Baskerville 11/12 pt
Printed in Great Britain by The Garden City Press,
Letchworth, Herts,
for the Publishers, B. T. Batsford Ltd,
4 Fitzhardinge Street, London W1H 0AH

ISBN 0 7134 1414 6

Contents

List of Illustrations

Edinburgh Castle. *Patrick Nasmyth*

Introduction

'Scotland', said Audubon, was 'made famous by the entrancing works of Sir Walter Scott'. Not only does that suggest the importance of Scott to his contemporaries and to Scotland, but it indicates the remoteness of Scotland from ordinary concerns of the time. Without Scott, Audubon also remarked, 'these beauties must perish unknown to the world'.

An anthologist's scan over the literary appreciation of Scottish landscape can now be more panoptic than Audubon's. Scottish writers were obviously stimulated by nature long before the vogue created by the Great Unknown. Apart from in the Border Ballads – quick, but vivid in their settings – there is a potent relish of nature in, for example, the Prologues of Gavin Douglas's *Eneados*, the first vernacular translation of Vergil's *Aeneid* which Douglas finished in the July of 1513.

> The frosty regioun ringis of the year,
> The time and season bitter, cald and paill,
> The short days that clerkis clepe brumaill,
> When brim blastis of the northern airt
> Owrwhelmit had Neptunus in his cairt,
> And all to-shaik the levis of the treis,
> The rageand storm owrweltrand wally seas.

Winter is sometimes thought to be the most deeply felt of Scottish seasons in literature and art. But that is an unsafe generalisation, for although it accorded well with the tragic narratives of mediaeval and renaissance poetry, there is, on the other hand, Hume's delightful evocation of midsummer day in *Of the Day Estivall* which, if of the period of James VI and therefore later, still complicates the issue.

Thomson's *The Seasons*, though later still by more than a

century, not only suggests a line of effectively universalised treatments of nature in which Scottish poets worked with distinction, but also marks the end of a long worked-out pastoral convention within which observation was removed from particularity.

There was no naming of places, and no need for it. Faith and speculation are as important as any other factors in attributing Thomson's *Winter* to memories of what he observed in his childhood and youth as a son of the manse in Roxburghshire. Interestingly enough, it was the first part of *The Seasons* to be published, in 1726, although expanded and revised in subsequent editions. His Juvenilia, while pastoral, are not particular either. Given Denham's *Cooper's Hill* or Pope's *Windsor Forest*, they could have been, with no loss of classical milieu involved.

In a subject like literary landscape, it is hard to escape the fact that it develops in strict parallel with convention. Nature is associated with feeling, and with intellect, as of the essence of the times, and with fashionable assuagements of the hunger of the spirit. Today's style of looking at landscapes is conditioned by ecological urgency. There is so much of it on television and in the newspapers and magazines that we may easily have forgotten the extent to which it forms a new style of observation, as important, perhaps, as the artificial manner of pastoral, or the romanticised grandeur and moods of Scott.

Fergusson, the fine and still neglected Scottish poet of eighteenth-century Edinburgh, was urbane and urban, classically pastoral when he wrote of nature, vigorous, satirical and vernacular when he described his town. Burns, his successor, was a country poet *par excellence*, but not in such a way that an anthologist of landscapes can find especially useful. A wise critic once observed of Burns's taste in scenery that 'he would have been completely at home in Surrey'. Labouring on the land, equipped with the tools of eighteenth-century Scottish agriculture, and paying rent for the privilege of it, can easily be imagined as having left Robert Burns with little inclination to indulge in a love of 'views', or a taste in the picturesque which, by 1776, the sketcher William Gilpin was attending to in Scotland along an itinerary which was thorough and influential on those of his countrymen who came after him. Burns's scenes are very much at the service of local loyalties, which, of course, endeared him to the mawkish parochialism on which his reputation was raised to the status of cult. His settings are there for the emplacement of events, especially amorous ones – the recollection of loves lost or postponed. His landscapes are humanised into backdrops for memory, friendships and recreation.

Although Thomson picked up no sense of particularity from Pope and Denham, a Scottish poet who did his best to do just that was John Wilson. Reams of Augustan-ised verse exist in the canon of Scottish poetry – justifiably neglected, indeed, and reading now more like attempts to lose a Scottish accent in pretentious elocutions than like poetry. Wilson, however, was working on the right lines, although his pastoral poem *Clyde* falls far short of the smooth artistry of his models. Handicapped by a lack of genius, which is crippling enough, his career ended when he took the position of headmaster of the Greenock Grammar School, where the interviewing committee bonded him by a legal and ecclesiastical document to leave over forever 'the profane and unprofitable art of poem-making'. Such was the attitude of the Kirk outside the more enlightened cities of Scotland.

Scott's landscapes are drawn with a remarkable gift of historical and pictorial imagination. Successive generations of tourists were seduced by his poems and novels to visit the scenes in which his tales were set. How many now arrive at The Trossachs with a copy of *The Lady of the Lake* in their pockets is anybody's guess, but I imagine they are very few indeed, for all the Rob Robbery and Walter Scottery to be seen in the names of the local hostelries.

Scott was a patriot of Scottish landscapes and of the history they had endured, either in fact or in his imagination. At the same time he was a patriarch of exactly that kind of politics, a by-product of which is the submergence of Scottish identity in the idea of North Britain, or Scotshire. Scott, in brief words, was a Unionist of the first water. Curiously, his romanticised landscapes and histories have in all likelihood contributed as much towards retarding that process as his political beliefs added to its advancement. Since Scott's time, many Scottish poets and writers have offered their tokens of national affection in the form of *un peu d'histoire* or interpretations of landscapes.

Before the eighteenth century literary visitors to Scotland were few and far between. At certain times, of course, it would have been literally dangerous. Sir Henry Wotton visited, but wrote nothing of it. Ben Jonson visited and wrote 'On his Picture left in Scotland', although as his friend Drummond of Hawthornden wrote only one poem at all relevant to my subject here, Jonson can hardly be despised for having said nothing of the sights he saw.

Indeed, there is considerable frustration in searching for verses written by literary strangers to Scotland. Defoe spent a good deal of time north of the Tweed, and wrote importantly of it in prose and verse. He was perhaps the most gifted spy and propagandist who ever lived. Carrying out his brief to excite the Scots into acceptance of the benefits of the Union of 1707, he wrote two poems in couplets. The first is pure flattery, as is the second, although this, *A Scots Poem*, is a more pointed recommendation to the Scots to take up the political, commercial and military advantages of the Treaty dangled before them by English opportunists and Scottish plutocrats. It is a remarkable document, but says nothing of landscape.

By about a hundred years later Thomas Love Peacock was writing his rombustious satires of Scotsmen's gifts for making financial successes of themselves – the 'Paper Money Lyrics'. It must, I suppose, be mentioned that English versifiers, whether in literary satire, or in the cruder but no less effective broadsides peddled on city streets, were a good deal more anti-Scots than, say, Collins in his 'Ode on the Popular Superstitions of the Highlands of Scotland' – highlands which he never visited. If nothing else, the opening up of Scottish scenery to tourism gave English poets a more favourable aspect of Scotland to write about.

'Scotland', said the American philosopher-poet, Emerson, 'was a camp before Culloden'. It is a wearily ignorant view of Scottish culture although, again, it serves to show how remote and little understood Scotland was until comparatively recent times. Foreign travellers would be concerned with diplomatic or commercial business before 1746, or else they came in uniform to the tap of the drum. But before Scott the influential hokum of Macpherson's Ossian had radiated forth like 'flu and into the psyches of European poets. Klopstock, Herder, Schiller, and even Goethe, were touched by it. Hugo, Musset and Vigny were affected in France, where it found an admirer in Napoleon, for whom Ingres painted his superbly vulgar picture of 'The Dream of Ossian' – to decorate a bed-chamber! Meeting this picture in the Musée Ingres at Montauban is a chastening lesson for a Scotsman, whose culture has been largely exported in the triumvirate of Macpherson's Ossian, Burns and Scott. All three went out of Scotland like chilly northern exotica, a misty, couthy or warlike version of *chinoiserie*.

Johnson's and Boswell's tour was imitated by others anxious to stand where the Great Cham had stood. Itineraries became established. In 1803, 1814 and 1831, Wordsworth toured and from his travels composed some forty poems. Those of 1803 are the best, particularly 'The Solitary Reaper', which, if hardly a landscape poem, is included here because it appears to assume the presence of the place as well as its girl. It is, in fact, an eminently Wordsworthian poem.

It is too much to ask of a poet that his talent be entirely transportable into new lands. What Keats was looking for in Scotland, I am not quite sure. Yet the opportunity of witnessing a different style of nature, and different customs, excited him. Interested readers should look up his letters of the time, in which, for instance, he is bitterly forthright about the sentimental misuse of Burns's birthplace, and he is not above a few generalisations on Scottish character, either:

A Scotchman's motive is more easily discovered
than an Irishman's. A Scotchman will go wisely
about to deceive you, an Irishman cunningly.

Later in the nineteenth century Scotland was firmly established on the map of desirable places to visit. Clough's remarkable poem 'The Bothie of Tober-na-Vuolich' – óne of the virtuoso pieces of the century – is based on a recreation of a Victorian reading-party of Oxford undergraduates, led by Clough himself. Victorian Scotland became *eminently* Victorian. Baronial halls, sporting trips for the hunter, angler or golfer, the Landseerisation of its scenery, all contributed to its new Balmoral and royal image. Famous Americans visited. Washington Irving came and was thoroughly disappointed. Francis Parkman, the great historian of the Indian wars, who had lived rough in the Rocky Mountains of the 1850s, came, and was thoroughly impressed, claiming that Irving was wildly wrong. Hawthorne came in the 1850s and got soaked at Inversnaid; he supposed he must have experienced a true Scotch mist. Emerson visited Carlyle, and in 1873 Mark Twain visited Dr John Brown in Edinburgh, whose elegy was written by R. L. Stevenson. Stephen Crane came north by train and, in 'The Scotch Express' wrote this of entering Glasgow:

A long, prison-like row of tenements, not at all
resembling London, but in one way resembling
New York, appeared to the left, and then sank out
of sight like a phantom.

Crane's little journalistic exercise in some ways prefigures W. H. Auden's vivid and exciting poem 'Night Mail'. Auden taught at Larchfield School in Helensburgh, as, too, did Cecil Day Lewis. If Lewis wrote anything of Scottish subjects, he never printed it, which suggests how, by the time of the modern and contemporary poets, the particular nature of a talent might not be so easily at home in surroundings new to it. Landscape poetry often has the mark of the occasional about it, and, certainly, the art of verse in the twentieth century seldom approves of that. But then we do have a poem by Eliot.

Douglas Dunn

Abbotsford. *From an engraving by T. Barber after T. H. Shepherd*

SCOTLAND

Here in the uplands
The soil is ungrateful;
The fields, red with sorrel,
Are stony and bare.
A few trees, wind-twisted —
Or are they but bushes? —
Stand stubbornly guarding
A home here and there.

Scooped out like a saucer,
The land lies before me,
The waters, once scattered,
Flow orderly now
Through fields where the ghosts
Of the marsh and the moorland
Still ride the old marches,
Despising the plough.

The marsh and the moorland
Are not to be banished;
The bracken and heather,
The glory of broom,
Usurp all the balks
And the field's broken fringes,
And claim from the sower
Their portion of room.

This is my country,
The land that begat me.
These windy spaces
Are surely my own.
And those who here toil
In the sweat of their faces
Are flesh of my flesh
And bone of my bone.

Hard is the day's task –
Scotland, stern Mother! –
Wherewith at all times
Thy sons have been faced.–
Labour by day,
And scant rest in the gloaming
With want an attendant
Not lightly outpaced.

Yet do thy children
Honour and love thee,
Harsh is thy schooling
Yet great is the gain.
True hearts and strong limbs,
The beauty of faces
Kissed by the wind
And caressed by the rain.

Sir Alexander Gray (1882–1967)

THE PRINCESS OF SCOTLAND

'Who are you that so strangely woke,
    And raised a fine hand?'
Poverty wears a scarlet cloke
        In my land.

'Duchies of dreamland, emerald, rose
    Lie at your command?'
Poverty like a princess goes
        In my land.

'Wherefore the mask of silken lace
    Tied with a golden band?'
Poverty walks with wanton grace
        In my land.

'Why do you softly, richly speak
    Rhythm so sweetly-scanned?'
Poverty hath the Gaelic and Greek
        In my land.

'There's a far-off scent about you seems
    Born in Samarkand.'
Poverty hath luxurious dreams
        In my land.

'You have wounds that like passion-flowers you hide:
    I cannot understand.'
Poverty hath one name with Pride
        In my land.

'Oh! Will you draw your last sad breath
    'Mid bitter bent and sand?'
Poverty begs from none but Death
        In my land.

                    Rachel Annand Taylor (1876–1960)

The Departure of the 'Night Scotsman'

22

NIGHT MAIL

North, north, north,
To the country of the Clyde and the Firth of Forth.

This is the night mail crossing the border,
Bringing the cheque and the postal order,
Letters for the rich, letters for the poor,
The shop at the corner and the girl next door.

Through sparse counties she rampages,
Her driver's eye upon her gages.
Panting up past lonely farms,
Fed by the fireman's restless arms.
Uplands heaped like slaughtered horses,
Rushing stony water courses,
Lurching through the cutting, and beneath the bridge,
Into the gap in the distant ridge.
Winding up the valley and the water-shed
Through the heather and the weather and the dawn overhead.
Pulling up Beattock, a steady climb –
The gradient's against her, but she's on time.

Past cotton grass and moorland boulder,
Shovelling white steam over her shoulder,
Snorting noisily as she passes
Silent miles of wind-bent grasses;
Birds turn their heads as she approaches,
Stare from the bushes at her blank-faced coaches;
Sheepdogs cannot turn her course,
They slumber on with paws across,
In the farm she passes no one wakes,
But a jug in a bedroom gently shakes.

Dawn freshens, the climb is done.
The train tilts forward for the downhill run.
Down towards Glasgow she descends
Towards the steam tugs, yelping down the glade of cranes.

Towards the fields of apparatus, the furnaces
Set on the dark plain like gigantic chessmen.
All Scotland waits for her.
Yes, this country, whose scribbled coastline traps the wild Atlantic
    in a maze of stone,
And faces Norway with its doubled notches.
In the dark glens, beside the pale-green sea-lochs,
Men long for news.

Letters of thanks, letters from banks,
Letters of joy from the girl and boy,
Receipted bills and invitations
To inspect new stock or visit relations,
And applications for situations,
And timid lovers' declarations,
And gossip, gossip from all the nations;
News circumstantial, news financial,
Letters with holiday snaps to enlarge in,
Letters with faces scrawled in the margin,
Letters from uncles, cousins and aunts,
Letters to Scotland from the South of France,
Letters of condolence to Highlands and Lowlands,
Notes from overseas to the Hebrides;
Written on paper of every hue,
The pink, the violet, the white and the blue.
The chatty, the catty, the boring, adoring,
The cold and official and the heart's outpouring,
Clever, stupid, short and long,
The typed and the printed and the spelt all wrong.

Thousands are still asleep
Dreaming of terrifying monsters
Or a friendly tea beside the band at Cranston's or Crawford's;
Asleep in working Glasgow, asleep in well-set Edinburgh,
Asleep in granite Aberdeen.
In grimed Dundee that weaves a white linen from the Indian fibre,
In Stornoway smoking its heavy wools,
And where the rivers feel the long salmon threshing in their
    netted mouths,
They continue their dreams,
But shall wake soon and long for letters.
And none will hear the postman's knock
Without a quickening of the heart,
For who can bear to feel himself forgotten?

W. H. Auden (1907–1973)
(Longer version, from *The English Auden*, 1977)

SUNSET PLOUGHING

The ploughhorse leaning through the red haze
shuttles also a field without fences,
a gay one, mine. I keep it
inside my skull.

Close up:
his chest gleams, his head
hammers; dragonish steam
jets down from his nostrils.

Long shot:
on the field of my mind
reddening towards another sunset
he shuttles, across and back across,
adding rib after rib
to that black corduroy.

Norman MacCaig (1910–   )

'December Ploughing'. *James McIntosh Patrick*

WINTER

from: The seasons

Now, when the cheerless empire of the sky
To Capricorn the Centaur Archer yields,
And fierce Aquarius stains th' inverted year;
Hung o'er the farthest verge of heaven, the Sun
Scarce spreads through ether the dejected day.
Faint are his gleams, and ineffectual shoot
His struggling rays, in horizontal lines
Through the thick air, as, clothed in cloudy storm,
Weak, wan, and broad, he skirts the southern sky,
And, soon descending, to the long dark night,
Wide-shading all, the prostrate world resigns.
Nor is the night unwish'd; while vital heat,
Light, life, and joy, the dubious day forsake.

Meantime, in sable cincture, shadows vast,
Deep-tinged and damp, and congregated clouds,
And all the vapoury turbulence of heaven,
Involve the face of things. Thus Winter falls,
A heavy gloom oppressive o'er the world,
Through Nature shedding influence malign,
And rouses up the seeds of dark disease.
The soul of Man dies in him, loathing life,
And black with more than melancholy views.
The cattle droop and o'er the furrowed land,
Fresh from the plough, the dun discoloured flocks,
Untended, spreading, crop the wholesome root.
Along the woods, along the moorish fens,
Sighs the sad Genius of the coming storm:
And up among the loose disjointed cliffs,
And fractured mountains wild, the brawling brook,
And cave, presageful, send a hollow moan,
Resounding long in listening Fancy's ear.

Then comes the father of the tempest forth,
Wrapt in black glooms. First joyless rains obscure
Drive through the mingling skies with vapours foul;
Dash on the mountain's brow, and shake the woods,
That grumbling wave below. Th' unsightly plain
Lies a brown deluge, as the low-bent clouds
Pour flood on flood, yet unexhausted still
Combine, and deepening into night, shut up
The day's fair face. The wanderers of heaven
Each to his home retire; save those that love
To take their pastime in the troubled air,
Or skimming flutter round the dimply pool.
The cattle from th' untasted fields return,
And ask, with meaning low, their wonted stalls,
Or ruminate in the contiguous shade.
Thither the household feathery people crowd,
The crested cock, with all his female train,
Pensive, and dripping; while the cottage-hind
Hangs o'er th' enlivening blaze, and taleful there
Recounts his simple frolic. Much he talks,
And much he laughs; nor recks the storm that blows
Without, and rattles on his humble roof.
    Wide o'er the brim, with many a torrent swelled,
And the mixed ruin of its banks o'erspread,
At last the roused-up river pours along.
Resistless, roaring, dreadful, down it comes
From the rude mountain and the mossy wild,
Tumbling through rocks abrupt, and sounding far;
Then o'er the sanded valley floating spreads,
Calm, sluggish, silent; till again, constrained
Between two meeting hills, it bursts away,
Where rocks and woods o'erhang the turbid stream;
There, gathering triple force, rapid, and deep,
It boils and wheels and foams, and thunders through.
    Nature! great parent! whose unceasing hand
Rolls round the Seasons of the changeful year,

How mighty, how majestic, are thy works!
With what a pleasing dread they swell the soul!
That sees astonished, and astonished sings.
Ye too, ye winds! that now begin to blow
With boisterous sweep, I raise my voice to you.
Where are your stores, ye powerful beings! say,
Where your aërial magazines reserved,
To swell the brooding terrors of the storm?

James Thomson (1700–1748)

'Loch Coruisk and the Cuchullin Mountains, Isle of Skye'.
George Fennel Robson

Ashestiel. *From an engraving by J. Horsburgh after J. M. W. Turner*

32

'BY LONE SAINT MARY'S SILENT LAKE . . .'

from: Marmion, Introduction to Canto II

Thou know'st it well, – nor fen, nor sedge,
Pollute the pure lake's crystal edge;
Abrupt and sheer, the mountains sink
At once upon the level brink;
And just a trace of silver sand
Marks where the water meets the land.
Far in the mirror, bright and blue,
Each hill's huge outline you may view;
Shaggy with heath, but lonely bare,
Nor tree, nor bush, nor brake, is there,
Save where, of land, yon slender line
Bears thwart the lake the scatter'd pine,
Yet even this nakedness has power,
And aids the feeling of the hour:
Nor thicket, dell, nor copse you spy,
Where living thing conceal'd might lie;
Nor point, retiring, hides a dell,
Where swain, or woodman lone, might dwell;
There's nothing left to fancy's guess,
You see that all is loneliness:
And silence aids – though the steep hills
Send to the lake a thousand rills;
In summer tide, so soft they weep,
The sound but lulls the ear asleep;
Your horse's hoof-tread sounds too rude,
So stilly is the solitude.

Sir Walter Scott (1771–1832)

YARROW VISITED

And is this – Yarrow? – *This* the Stream
Of which my fancy cherished,
So faithfully, a waking dream?
An image that hath perished!
O that some Minstrel's harp were near,
To utter notes of gladness,
And chase this silence from the air,
That fills my heart with sadness!

Yet why? – a silvery current flows
With uncontrolled meanderings;
Nor have these eyes by greater hills
Been soothed, in all my wanderings.
And, through her depths, Saint Mary's Lake
Is visibly delighted;
For not a feature of those hills
Is in the mirror slighted.

A blue sky bends o'er Yarrow vale,
Save where that pearly whiteness
Is round the rising sun diffused,
A tender hazy brightness;
Mild dawn of promise! that excludes
All profitless dejection;
Though not unwilling here to admit
A pensive recollection.

Where was it that the famous Flower
Of Yarrow Vale lay bleeding?
His bed perchance was yon smooth mound
On which the herd is feeding:
And haply from this crystal pool,
Now peaceful as the morning,
The Water-wraith ascended thrice –
And gave his doleful warning.

Delicious is the lay that sings
The haunt of happy Lovers,
The path that leads them to the grove,
The leafy grove that covers:
And pity sanctifies the Verse
That paints, by strength of sorrow,
The unconquerable strength of love;
Bear witness, rueful Yarrow!

But thou, that didst appear so fair
To fond imagination,
Dost rival in the light of day
Her delicate creation:
Meek loveliness is round thee spread,
A softness still and holy;
The grace of forest charms decayed,
And pastoral melancholy.

That region left, the vale unfolds
Rich groves of lofty stature,
With Yarrow winding through the pomp
Of cultivated nature;
And, rising from those lofty groves,
Behold a ruin hoary!
The shattered front of Newark's Towers,
Renowned in Border story.

Fair scenes for childhood's opening bloom,
For sportive youth to stray in;
For manhood to enjoy his strength;
And age to wear away in!
Yon cottage seems a bower of bliss,
A covert for protection
Of tender thoughts, that nestle there –
The brood of chaste affection.

Melrose Abbey. *James Ward*

36

How sweet on this autumnal day,
The wild-wood fruits to gather,
And on my True-love's forehead plant
A crest of blooming heather!
And what if I enwreathed my own!
'Twere no offence to reason;
The sober Hills thus deck their brows
To meet the wintry season.

I see – but not by sight alone,
Loved Yarrow, have I won thee;
A ray of fancy still survives –
Her sunshine plays upon thee!
Thy ever-youthful waters keep
A course of lively pleasure;
And gladsome notes my lips can breathe,
Accordant to the measure.

The vapours linger round the Heights,
They melt, and soon must vanish;
One hour is theirs, no more is mine –
Sad thought, which I would banish,
But that I know, where'er I go,
Thy genuine image, Yarrow!
Will dwell with me – to heighten joy,
And cheer my mind in sorrow.

William Wordsworth (1770–1850)

NOVEMBER

from: Marmion, Introduction to Canto I

November's sky is chill and drear,
November's leaf is red and sear:
Late, gazing down the steepy linn,
That hems our little garden in,
Low in its dark and narrow glen,
You scarce the rivulet might ken,
So thick the tangled greenwood grew,
So feeble trill'd the streamlet through:
Now, murmuring hoarse, and frequent seen
Through bush and brier, no longer green,
An angry brook, it sweeps the glade,
Brawls over rock and wild cascade,
And, foaming brown with double speed,
Hurries its waters to the Tweed.

   No longer Autumn's glowing red
Upon our Forest hills is shed;
No more, beneath the evening beam,
Fair Tweed reflects their purple gleam;
Away hath pass'd the heather-bell
That bloom'd so rich on Needpath-fell;
Sallow his brow, and russet bare
Are now the sister-heights of Yare.
The sheep, before the pinching heaven,
To shelter'd dale and down are driven,
Where yet some faded herbage pines,
And yet a watery sunbeam shines:
In meek despondency they eye
The wither'd sward and wintry sky,
And far beneath their summer hill,
Stray sadly by Glenkinnon's rill:
The shepherd shifts his mantle's fold,
And wraps him closer from the cold;

'Winter in Perthshire'. *James McIntosh Patrick*

His dogs no merry circles wheel,
But, shivering, follow at his heel;
A cowering glance they often cast,
As deeper moans the gathering blast.

My imps, though hardy, bold, and wild
As best befits the mountain child,
Feel the sad influence of the hour,
And wail the daisy's vanish'd flower;
Their summer gambols tell, and mourn,
And anxious ask, – Will spring return,
And birds and lambs again be gay,
And blossoms clothe the hawthorn spray?

Yes, prattlers, yes. The daisy's flower
Again shall paint your summer bower;
Again the hawthorn shall supply
The garlands you delight to tie;
The lambs upon the lea shall bound,
The wild birds carol to the round,
And while you frolic light as they,
Too short shall seem the summer day.

To mute and to material things
New life revolving summer brings;
The genial call dead Nature hears,
And in her glory reappears.
But oh! my Country's wintry state
What second spring shall renovate?

Sir Walter Scott (1771–1832)

40

A SONG ABOUT MYSELF

(written in Kirkcudbright)

I

There was a naughty boy,
  A naughty boy was he,
He would not stop at home,
  He could not quiet be –
    He took
    In his knapsack
    A book
    Full of vowels
    And a shirt
    With some towels,
    A slight cap
    For night-cap,
    A hair brush,
    Comb ditto,
    New stockings,
    For old ones
    Would split O!
    This knapsack
    Tight at's back
    He rivetted close
And followed his nose
    To the north,
    To the north,
And followed his nose
    To the north.

II

There was a naughty boy,
  And a naughty boy was he,
For nothing would he do
  But scribble poetry –
    He took
    An inkstand
    In his hand,
    And a pen
    Big as ten
    In the other.
    And away
    In a pother
    He ran
    To the mountains
    And fountains
    And ghostès
    And postès
    And witches
    And ditches,
    And wrote
    In his coat
    When the weather
    Was cool –
    Fear of gout –
    And without
    When the weather
    Was warm.
    Och, the charm
    When we choose
  To follow one's nose
    To the north,
    To the north,
  To follow one's nose
    To the north!

III

There was a naughty boy,
  And a naughty boy was he,
He kept little fishes
  In washing tubs three.
    In spite
    Of the might
    Of the maid,
    Nor afraid
    Of his granny-good,
    He often would
    Hurly burly
    Get up early
    And go,
    By hook or crook,
    To the brook
    And bring home
    Miller's thumb,
    Tittlebat
    Not over fat,
    Minnows small
    As the stall
    Of a glove,
    Not above
    The size
    Of a nice
    Little baby's
    Little finger –
    Oh, he made
    ('Twas his trade)
  Of fish a pretty kettle –
    A kettle,
    A kettle,
  Of fish a pretty kettle,
    A kettle!

IV

There was a naughty boy,
  And a naughty boy was he,
He ran away to Scotland
  The people for to see –
    Then he found
    That the ground
    Was as hard,
    That a yard
    Was as long,

That a song
Was as merry,
That a cherry
Was as red,
That lead
Was as weighty,
That fourscore
Was as eighty,
That a door
Was as wooden

As in England –
So he stood in his shoes
And he wondered,
He wondered,
He stood in his shoes
And he wondered.

John Keats (1795–1821)

Kirkcudbright. *From an engraving by W. Richardson after D. O. Hill*

Burns' Cottage. *From an engraving by T. J. Kelley after D. O. Hill*

44

SONNET

written in the cottage where Burns was born

This mortal body of a thousand days
  Now fills, O Burns, a space in thine own room,
Where thou didst dream alone on budded bays,
  Happy and thoughtless of thy day of doom!

My pulse is warm with thine own barley-bree,
  My head is light with pledging a great soul,
My eyes are wandering and I cannot see,
  Fancy is dead and drunken at its goal.
Yet can I stamp my foot upon thy floor,
  Yet can I ope thy window-sash to find
The meadow thou hast trampèd o'er and o'er,
  Yet can I think of thee till thought is blind,
Yet can I gulp a bumper to thy name –
Oh, smile among the shades, for this is fame!

John Keats (1795–1821)

AFTON WATER

Flow gently, sweet Afton, among thy green braes,
Flow gently, I'll sing thee a song in thy praise;
My Mary's asleep by thy murmuring stream,
Flow gently, sweet Afton, disturb not her dream.

Thou stock dove whose echo resounds thro' the glen,
Ye wild whistling blackbirds in yon thorny den,
Thou green crested lapwing thy screaming forbear,
I charge you disturb not my slumbering Fair.

How lofty, sweet Afton, thy neighbouring hills,
Far mark'd with the courses of clear, winding rills;
There daily I wander as noon rises high,
My flocks and my Mary's sweet Cot in my eye.

How pleasant thy banks and green vallies below,
Where wild in the woodlands the primroses blow;
There oft as mild ev'ning weeps over the lea,
The sweet scented birk shades my Mary and me.

Thy chrystal stream, Afton, how lovely it glides,
And winds by the cot where my Mary resides;
How wanton thy waters her snowy feet lave,
As gathering sweet flowerets she stems thy clear wave.

Flow gently, sweet Afton, among thy green braes,
Flow gently, sweet River, the theme of my lays;
My Mary's asleep by thy murmuring stream,
Flow gently, sweet Afton, disturb not her dream.

Robert Burns (1759–1796)

Glen Afton. *From an engraving by W. Richardson after D. O. Hill*

Cora Linn. *Jacob More*

'THE FALLS OF CLYDE'

from: Clyde

Where ancient Corehouse hangs above the stream,
And far beneath the tumbling surges gleam,
Engulphed in crags the fretting river raves,
Chafed into foam resound his tortured waves.
With giddy heads we view the dreadful deep,
And cattle snort and tremble at the steep,
Where down at once the foaming waters pour,
And tottering rocks repel the deafening roar.
Viewed from below, it seems from heaven they fell;
Seen from above, they seem to sink to hell;
But when the deluge pours from every hill,
And Clyde's wide bed ten thousand torrents fill,
His rage the murmuring mountain streams augment,
Redoubled rage in rocks so closely pent.
Then shattered woods, with ragged roots uptorn,
And herds and harvests down the waves are borne.
Huge stones heaved upward through the boiling deep,
And rocks enormous thundering down the steep,
In swift descent, fixed rocks encountering, roar,
Crash as from slings discharged, and shake the shore.
    From that drear grot which bears thy sacred name,
Heroic Wallace, ever dear to fame,
Did I the terrors of the scene behold.
I saw the liquid snowy mountains rolled
Prone down the awful steep; I heard the din
That shook the hill, from caves that boiled within.
Then wept the rocks and trees, with dropping hair;
Thick mists ascending, loaded all the air,
Blotted the sun, obscured the shining day,
And washed the blazing noon at once away.
The wreck below, in wild confusion tossed,
Convolved in eddies or in whirlpools lost,
Is swept along, or dashed upon the coast.

John Wilson (1720–1789)

ODE TO LEVEN WATER

On Leven's banks, while free to rove
And tune the rural pipe to love,
I envied not the happiest swain
That ever trod the Arcadian plain.
    Pure stream, in whose transparent wave
My youthful limbs I wont to lave,
No torrents stain thy limpid source,
No rocks impede thy dimpling course,
That warbles sweetly o'er its bed,
With white, round, polished pebbles spread,
While, lightly poised, the scaly brood
In myriads cleave thy crystal flood –
The springing trout in speckled pride,
The salmon, monarch of the tide,
The ruthless pike intent on war,
The silver eel, and mottled par.
Devolving from thy parent lake,
A charming maze thy waters make,
By bowers of birch and groves of pine,
And edges flowered with eglantine.

    Still on thy banks, so gaily green,
May numerous herds and flocks be seen,
And lasses, chanting o'er the pail,
And shepherds, piping in the dale,
And ancient faith, that knows no guile,
And Industry, embrowned with toil,
And hearts resolved and hands prepared
The blessings they enjoy to guard.

                    Tobias Smollett (1721–1771)

'Highland Landscape'. *Alexander Nasmyth*

51

GLASGOW

Sing, Poet, 'tis a merry world;
That cottage smoke is rolled and curled
    In sport, that every moss
Is happy, every inch of soil; –
Before *me* runs a road of toil
    With my grave cut across.
Sing, trailing showers and breezy downs –
I know the tragic hearts of towns.

City! I am true son of thine;
Ne'er dwelt I where great mornings shine
    Around the bleating pens;
Ne'er by the rivulets I strayed,
And ne'er upon my childhood weighed
    The silence of the glens.
Instead of shores where ocean beats,
I hear the ebb and flow of streets.

Black Labour draws his weary waves,
Into their secret-moaning caves;
    But with the morning light,
That sea again will overflow
With a long weary sound of woe,
    Again to faint in night.
Wave am I in that sea of woes,
Which, night and morning, ebbs and flows.

I dwelt within a gloomy court,
Wherein did never sunbeam sport;
    Yet there my heart was stirr'd –
My very blood did dance and thrill,
When on my narrow window-sill,
    Spring lighted like a bird.
Poor flowers – I watched them pine for weeks,
With leaves as pale as human cheeks.

Afar, one summer, I was borne;
Through golden vapours of the morn,
        I heard the hills of sheep:
I trod with a wild ecstasy
The bright fringe of the living sea:
        And on a ruined keep
I sat, and watched an endless plain
Blacken beneath the gloom of rain.

O fair the lightly sprinkled waste,
O'er which a laughing shower has raced!
        O fair the April shoots!
O fair the woods on summer days,
While a blue hyacinthine haze
        Is dreaming round the roots!
In thee, O City! I discern
Another beauty, sad and stern.

Draw thy fierce streams of blinding ore,
Smite on a thousand anvils, roar
        Down to the harbour-bars;
Smoulder in smoky sunsets, flare
On rainy nights, with street and square
        Lie empty to the stars.
From terrace proud to alley base
I know thee as my mother's face.

When sunset bathes thee in his gold,
In wreaths of bronze thy sides are rolled,
        Thy smoke is dusky fire;
And, from the glory round thee poured,
A sunbeam like an angel's sword
        Shivers upon a spire.
Thus have I watched thee, Terror! Dream!
While the blue Night crept up the stream.

The wild Train plunges in the hills,
He shrieks across the midnight rills;
    Streams through the shifting glare,
The roar and flap of foundry fires,
That shake with light the sleeping shires;
    And on the moorlands bare,
He sees afar a crown of light
Hang o'er thee in the hollow night.

At midnight, when thy suburbs lie
As silent as a noonday sky,
    When larks with heat are mute,
I love to linger on thy bridge,
All lonely as a mountain ridge,
    Disturbed but by my foot;
While the black lazy stream beneath,
Steals from its far-off wilds of heath.

And through thy heart, as through a dream,
Flows on that black disdainful stream;
    All scornfully it flows,
Between the huddled gloom of masts,
Silent as pines unvexed by blasts –
    'Tween lamps in streaming rows.
O wondrous sight! O stream of dread!
O long dark river of the dead!

Old Glasgow Bridge. *John Knox*

Afar, the banner of the year
Unfurls: but dimly prisoned here,
        'Tis only when I greet
A dropt rose lying in my way,
A butterfly that flutters gay
        Athwart the noisy street,
I know the happy Summer smiles
Around thy suburbs, miles on miles.

'Twere neither pæan now, nor dirge,
The flash and thunder of the surge
        On flat sands wide and bare;
No haunting joy or anguish dwells
In the green light of sunny dells,
        Or in the starry air.
Alike to me the desert flower,
The rainbow laughing o'er the shower.

While o'er thy walls the darkness sails,
I lean against the churchyard rails;
        Up in the midnight towers
The belfried spire, the street is dead,
I hear in silence over head
        The clang of iron hours:
It moves me not – I know her tomb
Is yonder in the shapeless gloom.

All raptures of this mortal breath,
Solemnities of life and death,
          Dwell in thy noise alone:
Of me thou hast become a part –
Some kindred with my human heart
          Lives in thy streets of stone;
For we have been familiar more
Than galley-slave and weary oar.

The beech is dipped in wine; the shower
Is burnished; on the swinging flower
          The latest bee doth sit.
The low sun stares through dust of gold,
And o'er the darkening heath and wold
          The large ghost-moth doth flit.
In every orchard Autumn stands,
With apples in his golden hands.

But all these sights and sounds are strange;
Then wherefore from thee should I range?
          Thou hast my kith and kin:
My childhood, youth, and manhood brave;
Thou hast that unforgotten grave
          Within thy central din.
A sacredness of love and death
Dwells in thy noise and smoky breath.

                    Alexander Smith (1830–1867)

'ON THE FIRTH OF CLYDE'

from: A Boy's Poem

... At length the stream
Broadened 'tween banks of daisies, and afar
The shadows flew upon the sunny hills;
And down the river, 'gainst the pale blue sky,
A town sat in its smoke. Look backward now!
Distance has stilled three hundred thousand hearts,
Drowned the loud roar of commerce, changed the proud
Metropolis which turns all things to gold,
To a thick vapour o'er which stands a staff
With smoky pennon streaming on the air.
Blotting the azure, too, we floated on,
Leaving a long and weltering wake behind.
And now the grand and solitary hills
That never knew the toil and stress of man,
Dappled with sun and cloud, rose far away.
My heart stood up to greet the distant land
Within the hollows of whose mountains lochs
Moan in their restless sleep; around whose peaks,
And scraggy islands ever dim with rain,
The lonely eagle flies. The ample stream
Widened into a sea. The boundless day
Was full of sunshine and divinest light,
And far above the region of the wind
The barred and rippled cirrus slept serene,
With combed and winnowed streaks of faintest cloud
Melting into the blue. A sudden veil
Of rain dimmed all; and when the shade drew off,
Before us, out toward the mighty sun,
The firth was throbbing with glad flakes of light.
The mountains from their solitary pines
Ran down in bleating pastures to the sea;
And round and round the yellow coasts I saw
Each curve and bend of the delightful shore
Hemmed with a line of villas white as foam.

On the Clyde. *Alexander Nasmyth*

Far off, the village smiled amid the light;
And on the level sands, the merriest troops
Of children sported with the laughing waves,
The sunshine glancing on their naked limbs.
White cottages, half smothered in rose blooms,
Peeped at us as we passed. We reached the pier,
Whence girls in fluttering dresses, shady hats,
Smiled rosy welcome. An impatient roar
Of hasty steam; from the broad paddles rushed
A flood of pale green foam, that hissed and freathed
Ere it subsided in the quiet sea.

Alexander Smith (1830–1867)

TO AILSA ROCK

Hearken, thou craggy ocean pyramid!
  Give answer from thy voice, the sea-fowls' screams!
  When were thy shoulders mantled in huge streams?
When from the sun was thy broad forehead hid?
How long is it since the mighty power bid
  Thee heave to airy sleep from fathom dreams –
  Sleep in the lap of thunder or sunbeams,
Or when grey clouds are thy cold coverlid?
Thou answer'st not, for thou art dead asleep.
  Thy life is but two dead eternities –
The last in air, the former in the deep,
  First with the whales, last with the eagle-skies.
Drowned wast thou till an earthquake made thee steep,
  Another cannot wake thy giant size.

John Keats (1795–1821)

Ailsa Craig. *From an engraving by P. Mazell after Moses Griffiths*

INVERSNAID

This darksome burn, horseback brown,
His rollrock highroad roaring down,
In coop and in comb the fleece of his foam
Flutes and low to the lake falls home.

And windpuff-bonnet of fáwn-fróth
Turns and twindles over the broth
Of a pool so pitchblack, féll-frówning,
It rounds and rounds Despair to drowning.

Degged with dew, dappled with dew
Are the groins of the braes that the brook treads through,
Wiry heathpacks, flitches of fern,
And the beadbonny ash that sits over the burn.

What would the world be, once bereft
Of wet and of wildness? Let them be left,
O let them be left, wildness and wet;
Long live the weeds and the wilderness yet.

Gerard Manley Hopkins (1844–1889)

'A Spate in the Highlands'. *T. S. Cooper*

LINES

written on visiting a scene in Argyleshire

At the silence of twilight's contemplative hour,
  I have mused in a sorrowful mood,
On the wind-shaken weeds that embosom the bower,
  Where the home of my forefathers stood.
All ruin'd and wild is their roofless abode,
  And lonely the dark raven's sheltering tree:
And travell'd by few is the grass-cover'd road,
Where the hunter of deer and the warrior trode
  To his hills that encircle the sea.

Yet wandering, I found on my ruinous walk,
  By the dial-stone aged and green,
One rose of the wilderness left on its stalk,
  To mark where a garden had been.
Like a brotherless hermit, the last of its race,
  All wild in the silence of nature, it drew,
From each wandering sun-beam, a lonely embrace
For the night-weed and thorn overshadow'd the place,
  Where the flower of my forefathers grew.

Sweet bud of the wilderness! emblem of all
  That remains in this desolate heart!
The fabric of bliss to its centre may fall,
  But patience shall never depart!
Though the wilds of enchantment, all vernal and bright,
  In the days of delusion by fancy combined
With the vanishing phantoms of love and delight,
Abandon my soul, like a dream of the night,
  And leave but a desert behind.

'The Morvern Hills from Crail, Argyllshire'. *James McIntosh Patrick*

64

Be hush'd, my dark spirit! for wisdom condemns
   When the faint and the feeble deplore;
Be strong as the rock of the ocean that stems
   A thousand wild waves on the shore!
Through the perils of chance, and the scowl of disdain,
   May thy front be unalter'd, thy courage elate!
Yea! even the name I have worshipp'd in vain
Shall awake not the sigh of remembrance again:
   To bear is to conquer our fate.

Thomas Campbell (1777–1844)

LUSS VILLAGE

Such walls, like honey, and the old are happy
in morphean air like gold-fish in a bowl.
Ripe roses trail their margins down a sleepy
mediaeval treatise on the slumbering soul.

And even the water, fabulously silent,
has no salt tales to tell us, nor makes jokes
about the yokel mountains, huge and patient,
that will not court her but read shadowy books.

A world so long departed! In the churchyard
the tilted tombs still gossip, and the leaves
of stony testaments are read by Richard,
Jean and Carol, pert among the sheaves

of unscythed shadows, while the noon day hums
with bees and water and the ghosts of psalms.

Iain Crichton Smith (1928–   )

'IN THE DEEP TROSSACHS...'

from: *The Lady of the Lake, Canto I*

The western waves of ebbing day
Roll'd o'er the glen their level way;
Each purple peak, each flinty spire,
Was bathed in floods of living fire.
But not a setting beam could glow
Within the dark ravines below,
Where twined the path in shadow hid,
Round many a rocky pyramid.
Shooting abruptly from the dell
Its thunder-splinter'd pinnacle;
Round many an insulated mass,
The native bulwarks of the pass,
Huge as the tower which builders vain
Presumptuous piled on Shinar's plain.
The rocky summits, split and rent,
Form'd turret, dome, or battlement,
Or seem'd fantastically set
With cupola or minaret,
Wild crests as pagod ever deck'd,
Or mosque of Eastern architect.
Nor were these earth-born castles bare,
Nor lack'd they many a banner fair;
For, from their shiver'd brows displayed,
Far, o'er the unfathomable glade,
All twinkling with the dewdrops sheen,
The brier-rose fell in streamers green,
And creeping shrubs, of thousand dyes,
Waved in the west-wind's summer sighs.

Boon nature scatter'd, free and wild,
Each plant or flower, the mountain's child.
Here eglantine embalm'd the air,
Hawthorn and hazel mingled there;
The primrose pale and violet flower,
Found in each cliff a narrow bower;

67

Fox-glove and night-shade, side by side,
Emblems of punishment and pride,
Group'd their dark hues with every stain
The weather-beaten crags retain.
With boughs that quaked at every breath,
Grey birch and aspen wept beneath;
Aloft, the ash and warrior oak
Cast anchor in the rifted rock;
And, higher yet, the pine-tree hung
His shatter'd trunk, and frequent flung,
Where seem'd the cliffs to meet on high,
His boughs athwart the narrow'd sky.

Highest of all, where white peaks glanced,
Where glist'ning streamers waved and danced,
The wanderer's eye could barely view
The summer heaven's delicious blue;
So wondrous wild, the whole might seem
The scenery of a fairy dream.
And now, to issue from the glen,
No pathway meets the wanderer's ken,
Unless he climb, with footing nice,
A far projecting precipice.
The broom's tough roots his ladder made,
The hazel saplings lent their aid;
And thus an airy point he won,
Where, gleaming with the setting sun,
One burnish'd sheet of living gold,
Loch Katrine lay beneath him roll'd,
In all her length far winding lay,
With promontory, creek, and bay,
And islands that, empurpled bright,
Floated amid the livelier light,
And mountains, that like giants stand,
To sentinel enchanted land.
High on the south, huge Benvenue
Down on the lake in masses threw
Crags, knolls, and mounds, confusedly hurl'd,
The fragments of an earlier world;
A wildering forest feather'd o'er
His ruin'd sides and summit hoar,
While on the north, through middle air,
Ben-an heaved high his forehead bare.

Sir Walter Scott (1771–1832)

Ben Arthur. *J. M. W. Turner*

THE SOLITARY REAPER

Behold her, single in the field,
Yon solitary Highland Lass!
Reaping and singing by herself;
Stop here, or gently pass!
Alone she cuts and binds the grain,
And sings a melancholy strain;
O listen! for the Vale profound
Is overflowing with the sound.

No Nightingale did ever chaunt
More welcome notes to weary bands
Of travellers in some shady haunt,
Among Arabian sands;
A voice so thrilling ne'er was heard
In spring-time from the Cuckoo-bird,
Breaking the silence of the seas
Among the farthest Hebrides.

Will no one tell me what she sings? –
Perhaps the plaintive numbers flow
For old, unhappy, far-off things,
And battles long ago:
Or is it some more humble lay,
Familiar matter of to-day?
Some natural sorrow, loss, or pain,
That has been, and may be again?

Whate'er the theme, the Maiden sang
As if her song could have no ending;
I saw her singing at her work,
And o'er the sickle bending: –
I listened, motionless and still;
And, as I mounted up the hill,
The music in my heart I bore,
Long after it was heard no more.

William Wordsworth (1770–1850)

70

'The Hind's Daughter'. *James Guthrie*

THE CUILLIN HILLS

Each step a cataract of stones
So that I rise and sink at once,
Slowly up to the ridge I creep;
And as through drifting smoke
Of mist grey-black as a hoodie-crow
The ghostly boulders come and go
And two hoarse ravens croak
That hopped with flapping wings by a dead sheep,
All is so hideous that I know
It would not kill me though I fell
A thousand feet below;
On you, Black Cuillin, I am now in hell.

Andrew Young (1885–1971)

GLEN ALMAIN

or The Narrow Glen

In this still place, remote from men,
Sleeps Ossian, in the NARROW GLEN;
In this still place, where murmurs on
But one meek streamlet, only one:
He sang of battles, and the breath
Of stormy war, and violent death;
And should, methinks, when all was past,
Have rightfully been laid at last
Where rocks were rudely heaped, and rent
As by a spirit turbulent;
Where sights were rough, and sounds were wild,
And everything unreconciled;
In some complaining, dim retreat,
For fear and melancholy meet;
But this is calm; there cannot be
A more entire tranquillity.

Does then the Bard sleep here indeed?
Or is it but a groundless creed?
What matters it? – I blame them not
Whose Fancy in this lonely Spot
Was moved; and in such a way expressed
Their notion of its perfect rest.
A convent, even a hermit's cell,
Would break the silence of this Dell:
It is not quiet, is not ease;
But something deeper far than these:
The separation that is here
Is of the grave; and of austere
Yet happy feelings of the dead:
And, therefore, was it rightly said
That Ossian, last of all his race!
Lies buried in this lonely place.

William Wordsworth (1770–1850)

RANNOCH, BY GLENCOE

Here the crow starves, here the patient stag
Breeds for the rifle. Between the soft moor
And the soft sky, scarcely room
To leap or soar. Substance crumbles, in the thin air
Moon cold or moon hot. The road winds in
Listlessness of ancient war,
Languor of broken steel,
Clamour of confused wrong, apt
In silence. Memory is strong
Beyond the bone. Pride snapped,
Shadow of pride is long, in the long pass
No concurrence of bone.

T. S. Eliot (1888–1965)

Glencoe. *Horatio McCulloch*

LOCH TORRIDON

The dawn of night more fair than morning rose,
Stars hurrying forth on stars, as snows on snows
Haste when the wind and winter bid them speed.
Vague miles of moorland road behind us lay
Scarce traversed ere the day
Sank, and the sun forsook us at our need,
Belated. Where we thought to have rested, rest
Was none; for soft Maree's dim quivering breast,
Bound round with gracious inland girth of green
And fearless of the wild wave-wandering West,
Shone shelterless for strangers; and unseen
The goal before us lay
Of all our blithe and strange and strenuous day.

For when the northering road faced westward – when
The dark sharp sudden gorge dropped seaward – then,
Beneath the stars, between the steeps, the track
We followed, lighted not of moon or sun,
And plunging whither none
Might guess, while heaven and earth were hoar and black,
Seemed even the dim still pass whence none turns back:
And through the twilight leftward of the way,
And down the dark, with many a laugh and leap,
The light blithe hill-streams shone from scaur to steep
In glittering pride of play;
And ever while the night grew great and deep
We felt but saw not what the hills would keep
Sacred awhile from sense of moon or star;
And full and far
Beneath us, sweet and strange as heaven may be,
The sea.

The very sea: no mountain-moulded lake
Whose fluctuant shapeliness is fain to take
Shape from the steadfast shore that rules it round,
And only from the storms a casual sound:

The sea, that harbours in her heart sublime
The supreme heart of music deep as time,
And in her spirit strong
The spirit of all imaginable song...

And the dawn leapt in at my casement: and there, as I rose, at
    my feet
No waves of the landlocked waters, no lake submissive and sweet,
Soft slave of the lordly seasons, whose breath may loose it or freeze;
But to left and to right and ahead was the ripple whose pulse is
    the sea's.

From the gorge we had travelled by starlight the sunrise, winged
    and aflame,
Shone large on the live wide wavelets that shuddered with joy as
    it came;
As it came and caressed and possessed them, till panting and
    laughing with light
From mountain to mountain the water was kindled and stung to
    delight.
And the grey gaunt heights that embraced and constrained and
    compelled it were glad,
And the rampart of rock, stark naked, that thwarted and barred
    it, was clad
With a stern grey splendour of sunrise: and scarce had I sprung
    to the sea
When the dawn and the water were wedded, the hills and the
    sky set free.
The chain of the night was broken. the waves that embraced me
    and smiled
And flickered and fawned in the sunlight, alive, unafraid, un-
    defiled,
Were sweeter to swim in than air, though fulfilled with the mount-
    ing morn,
Could be for the birds whose triumph rejoiced that a day was
    born.

And a day was arisen indeed for us. Years and the changes of years
Clothed round with their joys and their sorrows, and dead as their
    hopes and their fears,
Lie noteless and nameless, unlit by remembrance or record of days
Worth wonder or memory, or cursing or blessing, or passion or
    praise,
Between us who live and forget not, but yearn with delight in it
    yet,
And the day we forget not, and never may live and may think to
    forget.
And the years that were kindlier and fairer, and kindled with
    pleasures as keen,
Have eclipsed not with lights or with shadows the light on the
    face of it seen.
For softly and surely, as nearer the boat that we gazed from drew,
The face of the precipice opened and bade us as birds pass
    through,
And the bark shot sheer to the sea through the strait of the sharp
    steep cleft,
The portal that opens with imminent rampires to right and to
    left,
Sublime as the sky they darken and strange as a spell-struck
    dream,
On the world unconfined of the mountains, the reign of the sea
    supreme,
The kingdom of westward waters, wherein when we swam we
    knew
The waves that we clove were boundless, the wind on our brows
    that blew
Had swept no land and no lake, and had warred not on tower
    or on tree,
But came on us hard out of heaven, and alive with the soul of
    the sea.

Algernon Charles Swinburne (1837–1909)
(Abbreviated version)

from

THE BOTHIE OF
TOBER-NA-VUOLICH

Ut vidi, ut perii, ut me malus abstulit error

So in the golden weather they waited. But Philip returned not.
Sunday six days thence a letter arrived in his writing. –
But, O Muse, that encompassest Earth like the ambient ether,
Swifter than steamer or railway or magical missive electric
Belting like Ariel the sphere with the star-like trail of thy travel,
Thou with thy Poet, to mortals mere post-office second-hand
    knowledge
Leaving, wilt seek in the moorland of Rannoch the wandering
    hero.
    There is it, there, or in lofty Lochaber, where, silent upheaving,
Heaving from ocean to sky, and under snow-winds of September,
Visibly whitening at morn to darken by noon in the shining,
Rise on their mighty foundations the brethren huge of Ben-nevis?
There, or westward away, where roads are unknown to Loch
    Nevish,
And the great peaks look abroad over Skye to the westernmost
    islands?
There is it? there? or there, we shall find our wandering hero?
    Here, in Badenoch, here, in Lochaber anon, in Lochiel, in
Knoydart, Moydart, Morrer, Ardgower, and Ardnamurchan,
Here I see him and here: I see him; anon I lose him!
Even as cloud passing subtly unseen from mountain to mountain,
Leaving the crest of Ben-more to be palpable next on Ben-vohrlich
Or like to hawk of the hill which ranges and soars in its hunting,
Seen and unseen by turns, now here, now in ether cludent.
    Wherefore as cloud of Ben-more or hawk over-ranging the
    mountains,
Wherefore in Badenoch drear, in lofty Lochaber, Lochiel, and
Knoydart, Moydart, Morrer, Ardgower, and Ardnamurchan,
Wandereth he, who should either with Adam be studying logic,
Or by the lochside of Rannoch on Katie his rhetoric using;
He who, his three weeks past, past now long ago, to the cottage

Punctual promised return to cares of classes and classics,
He who, smit to the heart by that youngest comeliest daughter,
Bent, unregardful of spies, at her feet, spreading clothes from her
    wash-tub?
Can it be with him through Badenoch, Morrer, and Ardnamur-
    chan,
Can it be with him he beareth the golden-haired lassie of Ran-
    noch?

Rannoch Muir. *Horatio McCulloch*

This fierce, furious walking – o'er mountain-top and moorland,
Sleeping in shieling and bothie, with drover on hill-side sleeping,
Folded in plaid, where sheep are strewn thicker than rocks by
    Loch Awen,
This fierce, furious travel unwearying – cannot in truth be
Merely the wedding tour succeeding the week of wooing!

                Arthur Hugh Clough (1819–1861)

'A Highland Stream, Glenfruin'. *John Milne Donald*

IN THE HIGHLANDS

In the highlands, in the country places,
Where the old plain men have rosy faces,
    And the young fair maidens
        Quiet eyes:
Where essential silence cheers and blesses,
And for ever in the hill-recesses
    Her more lovely music
        Broods and dies.

O to mount again where erst I haunted;
Where the old red hills are bird-enchanted,
    And the low green meadows
        Bright with sward;
And when even dies, the million-tinted,
And the night has come, and planets glinted,
    Lo, the valley hollow
        Lamp-bestarred!

O to dream, O to awake and wander
There, and with delight to take and render,
    Through the trance of silence,
        Quiet breath;
Lo! for there, among the flowers and grasses,
Only the mightier movement sounds and passes;
    Only winds and rivers,
        Life and death.

Robert Louis Stevenson (1850–1894)

LACHIN Y GAIR

Away, ye gay landscapes, ye gardens of roses!
  In you let the minions of luxury rove;
Restore me the rocks, where the snowflake reposes,
  Though still they are sacred to freedom and love:
Yet, Caledonia, beloved are thy mountains,
  Round their white summits though elements war;
Though cataracts foam 'stead of smooth-flowing fountains,
  I sigh for the valley of dark Loch na Garr.

Ah! there my young footsteps in infancy wandered;
   My cap was the bonnet, my cloak was the plaid;
On chieftains long perish'd my memory ponder'd,
   As daily I strode through the pine-cover'd glade;
I sought not my home till the day's dying glory
   Gave place to the rays of the bright polar star;
For fancy was cheer'd by traditional story,
   Disclosed by the natives of dark Loch na Garr.

'North West View from Ben Lomond'. *John Knox*

'Shades of the dead! have I not heard your voices
   Rise on the night-rolling breath of the gale?'
Surely the soul of the hero rejoices,
   And rides on the wind, o'er his own Highland vale.
Round Loch na Garr while the stormy mist gathers,
   Winter presides in his cold icy car:
Clouds there encircle the forms of my fathers;
   They dwell in the tempests of dark Loch na Garr.

'Ill-starr'd, though brave, did no visions foreboding
   Tell you that fate had forsaken your cause?'
Ah! were you destined to die at Culloden,
   Victory crown'd not your fall with applause:
Still were you happy in death's early slumber,
   You rest with your clan in the caves of Braemar;
The pibroch resounds, to the piper's loud number,
   Your deeds on the echoes of dark Loch na Garr.

Years have roll'd on, Loch na Garr, since I left you,
   Years must elapse ere I tread you again:
Nature of verdure and flow'rs has bereft you,
   Yet still you are dearer than Albion's plain.
England! thy beauties are tame and domestic
   To one who has roved o'er the mountains afar:
Oh for the crags that are wild and majestic!
   The steep frowning glories of dark Loch na Garr.

                    Lord Byron (1788–1824)

WINTER IN STRATHEARN

The twinkling Earn, like a blade in the snow,
The low hills scalloped against the hill,
The high hills leaping upon the low,
And the amber wine in the cup of the sky,
With the white world creaming over the rim,
She watched; and a keen aroma rose,
Embodied, a star above the snows;
For when the west sky-edge grows dim,
When lights are silver and shades are brown,
Behind Torlum the sun goes down;
And from Glenartney, night by night;
The full fair star of evening creeps;
Though spectral branches clasp it tight,
Like magic from their hold it leaps,
And reaches heaven at once. Her sight
Gathers the star, and in her eyes
She meekly wears heaven's fairest prize.

John Davidson (1857–1909)

IONA

(Upon landing)

How sad a welcome! To each voyager
Some ragged child holds up for sale a store
Of wave-worn pebbles, pleading on the shore
Where once came monk and nun with gentle stir,
Blessings to give, news ask, or suit prefer.
Yet is yon neat trim church a grateful speck
Of novelty amid the sacred wreck
Strewn far and wide. Think, proud Philosopher!
Fallen though she be, this Glory of the west,
Still on her sons the beams of mercy shine;
And 'hopes, perhaps more heavenly bright than thine,
A grace by thee unsought and unpossest,
A faith more fixed, a rapture more divine
Shall gild their passage to eternal rest'.

William Wordsworth (1770–1850)

Iona Cathedral. *From an engraving by P. Mazell after Moses Griffiths*

LOCH LUICHART

Slioch and Sgurr Mor
Hang in the air in a white chastity
Of cloud and February snow
That less to earth they seem to owe
Than to the pale blue cloud-drift or
The deep blue sky.

Though high and far they stand,
Their shadows of leagues of forest come,
Here, to a purer beauty thinned
Is this true mirror, now the wind,
That held it with a shaking hand,
Droops still and dumb.

As I push from the shore
And drift (beneath that buzzard) I climb now
These silver hills for miles and miles,
Breaking hard rock to gentle smiles
With the slow motion of my prow
And dripping oar.

Andrew Young (1885–1971)

'NOT ALADDIN MAGIAN'

(Staffa)

Not Aladdin magian
Ever such a work began;
Not the wizard of the Dee
Ever such a dream could see;
Not St John in Patmos' Isle,
In the passion of his toil,
Gazed on such a rugged wonder.
As I stood its roofing under,
Lo! I saw one sleeping there
On the marble cold and bare,
While the surges washed his feet
And his garments white did beat,
Drenched, about the sombre rocks.
On his neck his well-grown locks,
Lifted dry above the main,
Were upon the curl again.
'What is this? and who art thou?'
Whispered I, and touched his brow.
'What art thou and what is this?'
Whispered I, and strove to kiss
The spirit's hand to wake his eyes.
Up he started in a trice.
'I am Lycidas,' said he,
'Famed in funeral minstrelsy!
This was architected thus
By the great Oceanus!
Here his mighty waters play
Hollow organs all the day;
Here by turns his dolphins all,
Finny palmers great and small,
Come to pay devotion due,
Each a mouth of pearls must strew.
Many mortals of these days
Dare to pass our sacred ways,
Dare to see audaciously

Staffa: Fingal's Cave. *From an engraving by Thomas Major after Moses Griffiths*

This Cathedral of the sea.
I have been the pontiff-priest
Where the waters never rest,
Where a fledgy sea-bird quire
Soars for ever; holy fire
Have I hid from mortal man;
Proteus is my sacristan.
But the stupid eye of mortal
Hath passed beyond the rocky portal,
So for ever will I leave
Such a taint and soon unweave
All the magic of the place –
'Tis now free to stupid face,
To cutters and to fashion boats,
To cravats and to petticoats.
The great sea shall war it down
For its fame shall not be blown
At every farthing quadrille dance.'
So saying with a spirit's glance
He dived ...

John Keats (1795–1821)

EALASAID

Here are the shores you loved,
The tumbling waters
Curling and foaming on Atlantic strands,
The ocean gentian-blue beyond believing,
The clean white sands.

And here the ancient speech
You loved essaying,
Rising and falling like the wave-borne birds;
The cadences that wind and tide are weaving
In Gaelic words.

And here the little crofts
With thatch stone-weighted
You told me of, so often ere I came.
How strange that I am here without you, grieving
Your lost, loved name.

O sleep you soundly now,
Ealasaid darling,
Beneath the sandy turf on Tiree's shore.
No more your island home you need be leaving,
Be sad no more.

Helen B. Cruickshank (1886–1975)

After the Launch: Scarpa, West Harris. *From a photograph by Robert M. Adam*

GLENARADALE

There is no fire of the crackling boughs
    On the hearths of our fathers,
There is no lowing of brown-eyed cows
    On the green meadows,
Nor do the maidens whisper vows
    In the still gloaming,
        Glenaradale.

There is no bleating of sheep on the hill
    Where the mists linger,
There is no sound of the low hand-mill
    Ground by the women,
And the smith's hammer is lying still
    By the brown anvil,
        Glenaradale.

Ah! we must leave thee and go away
    Far from Ben Luibh,
Far from the graves where we hoped to lay
    Our bones with our fathers',
Far from the kirk where we used to pray
    Lowly together,
        Glenaradale.

We are not going for hunger of wealth,
    For the gold and silver,
We are not going to seek for health
    On the flat prairies,
Nor yet for the lack of fruitful tilth
    On thy green pastures,
        Glenaradale.

Content with the croft and the hill were we,
    As all our fathers,
Content with the fish in the lake to be
    Carefully netted,
And garments spun of the wool from thee,
    O black-faced wether
        Of Glenaradale.

No father here but would give a son
    For the old country,
And his mother the sword would have girded on
    To fight her battles:
Many's the battle that has been won
    By the brave tartans,
        Glenaradale.

But the big-horn'd stag and his hinds, we know,
    In the high corries,
And the salmon that swirls in the pool below
    Where the stream rushes
Are more than the hearts of men, and so
    We leave thy green valley,
        Glenaradale.

Walter C. Smith (1824–1908)

MUSICAL MOMENT IN ASSYNT

A mountain is a sort of music: theme
And counter theme displaced in air amongst
Their own variations.
Wagnerian Devil signed the Ciogach score;
And God was Mozart when he wrote Cul Mor.

You climb a trio when you climb Cul Beag.
Stac Polly – there's a rondo in seven sharps,
Neat as a trivet.
And Quinag, rallentando in the haze,
Is one long tune extending phrase by phrase.

I listen with my eyes and see through that
Mellifluous din of shapes my masterpiece
Of masterpieces:
One sandstone chord that holds up time in space –
Sforzando Suilven reared on his ground bass.

Norman MacCaig (1910–   )

'Loch Avon and the Cairngorm Mountains'. *Sir Edwin Landseer*

'First Steamboat on the Clyde'. *John Knox*

CHILDHOOD

Long time he lay upon the sunny hill,
  To his father's house below securely bound.
Far off the silent, changing sound was still,
  With the black islands lying thick around.

He knew each separate height, each vaguer hue,
  Where the massed isles more distant rolled away;
But though all ran together in his view,
  He knew that unseen straits between them lay.

Sometimes he wondered what new shores were there:
  In thought he saw the still light on the sand,
The shallow water clear in tranquil air,
  And walked through it in joy from strand to strand.

Oft o'er the sound a ship so slow would pass
  That in the black hills' gloom it seemed to lie;
The evening sound was smooth like sunken glass,
  And time seemed finished ere the ship passed by.

Grey tiny rocks slept round him where he lay,
  Moveless as they; more still when evening came.
The grasses threw straight shadows far away,
  And from the house his mother called his name.

Edwin Muir (1887–1959)

ORKNEY CROFTER

Scant are the few green acres that I till,
But arched above them spreads the boundless sky,
   Ripening their crops; and round them lie
     Long miles of moorland hill.

Beyond the cliff-top glimmers in the sun
The far horizon's bright infinity;
   And I can gaze across the sea
     When my day's work is done.

The solitudes of land and sea assuage
My quenchless thirst for freedom unconfined;
   With independent heart and mind
     Hold I my heritage.

Robert Rendall (1898–1967)

'A Galloway Landscape'. *George Henry*

St Andrews. *Sam Bough*

ALMAE MATRES

(St Andrews, 1862. Oxford, 1865)

St Andrews by the northern sea,
  A haunted town it is to me!
A little city, worn and gray,
  The gray North Ocean girds it round;
And o'er the rocks, and up the bay,
  The long sea-rollers surge and sound;
And still the thin and biting spray
  Drives down the melancholy street,
And still endure, and still decay,
  Towers that the salt winds vainly beat.
Ghost-like and shadowy they stand
Dim-mirrored in the wet sea-sand.

O ruined chapel! long ago
  We loitered idly where the tall
Fresh-budded mountain-ashes blow
  Within thy desecrated wall:
The tough roots rent the tomb below,
  The April birds sang clamorous,
We did not dream, we could not know,
  How hardly fate would deal with us!

O broken minster, looking forth
  Beyond the bay, above the town!
O winter of the kindly North,
  O college of the scarlet gown,
And shining sands beside the sea,
  And stretch of links beyond the sand,
Once more I watch you, and to me
  It is as if I touched his hand!

And therefore art thou yet more dear,
    O little city, gray and sere,
Though shrunken from thine ancient pride
    And lonely by thy lonely sea,
Than these fair halls on Isis' side,
    Where Youth an hour came back to me!

A land of waters green and clear,
    Of willows and of poplars tall,
And, in the spring-time of the year,
    The white may breaking over all,
And Pleasure quick to come at call,
    And summer rides by marsh and wold,
And autumn with her crimson pall
    About the towers of Magdalen rolled;
And strange enchantments from the past,
    And memories of the friends of old,
And strong Tradition, binding fast
    The 'flying terms' with bands of gold,–

All these hath Oxford: all are dear,
    But dearer far the little town,
The drifting surf, the wintry year,
    The college of the scarlet gown,
        St Andrews by the northern sea,
        That is a haunted town to me!

Andrew Lang (1844–1912)

from

EDINBURGH

EDINA, high in heaven wan,
Towered, templed, Metropolitan,
    Waited upon by hills,
River and wide-spread ocean, tinged
By April light, or draped and fringed
    As April vapour wills –
Thou hangest, like a Cyclops' dream,
High in the shifting weather-gleam.

The spring-time stains with emerald
Thy Castle's precipices bald;
    Within thy streets and squares
The sudden summer camps, and blows
The plenteous chariot-shaken rose;
    Or, lifting unawares
My eyes from out thy central strife,
Lo, far off, harvest-brazen Fife!

Fair art thou, City, to the eye,
But fairer to the memory:
    There is no place that breeds –
Not Venice 'neath her mellow moons,
When the sea-pulse of full lagoons
    Waves all her palace weeds –
Such wistful thoughts of far away,
Of the eternal yesterday.

Within thy high-piled Canongate
The air is of another date;
    All speaks of ancient time:
Traces of gardens, dials, wells,
Thy dizzy gables, oyster-shells
    Imbedded in the lime –
Thy shields above the doors of peers
Are old as Mary Stuart's tears.

Great City, every morning I
See thy wild fringes in the sky,
    Soft-blurr'd with smoky grace:
Every evening note the blazing sun
Flush luridly thy vapours dun –
    A spire athwart his face:
Each night I watch thy wondrous feast,
Like some far city of the East.

But most I love thee faint and fair,
Dim-pencill'd in the evening air,
    When in the dewy bush
I hear from budded thick remote
The rapture of the blackbird's throat,
    The sweet note of the thrush;
And all is shadowless and clear
In the uncoloured atmosphere.

                Alexander Smith (1830–1866)

MONTROSE

Where better could a town be placed than here?
Peninsular Montrose has everything
With water on three sides, while, beyond
Rich farmlands, the hills upswing.

It has the right size too – not a huge
Sprawling mass, but compact as a heart,
Life-supplier to a whole diversified area
Yet with the economy of a work of art.

So small that it is possible to know
Everyone in it, yet it still radiates
In ties not broken but strengthened
To successive generations of expatriates.

So small and yet radiating out
Not only in space but in time, since here
History gives permanence of distinction
And dignity to each succeeding year.

'Guid gear gangs in sma' book' and fegs!
Man's story owes more to little towns than to great,
And Montrose is typical of Scotland's small grey burghs
Each with a character of its own time cannot abate.

Model of the preference of quality to quantity
Montrose set here between the hills and the sea
On its tongue of land is a perfect example
Of multum in parvo – Earth's best in epitome.

Hugh MacDiarmid (1892–1978)

FROM A WINDOW IN PRINCES STREET

Above the Crags that fade and gloom
Starts the bare knee of Arthur's Seat;
Ridged high against the evening bloom,
The Old Town rises, street on street;
With lamps bejewelled, straight ahead,
Like rampired walls the houses lean,
All spired and domed and turreted,
Sheer to the valley's darkling green;
Ranged in mysterious disarray,
The Castle, menacing and austere,
Looms through the lingering last of day;
And in the silver dusk you hear,
Reverberated from crag and scar,
Bold bugles blowing points of war.

W. E. Henley (1849–1903)

Edinburgh Castle. *Photograph: Judges*

Edinburgh from the Castle. *From an anonymous lithograph*

EDINBURGH

Midnight

Glasgow is null,
Its suburbs shadows
And the Clyde a cloud.

Dundee is dust
And Aberdeen a shell.

But Edinburgh is a mad god's dream,
Fitful and dark,
Unseizable in Leith
And wildered by the Forth,
But irresistibly at last
Cleaving to sombre heights
Of passionate imagining
Till stonily,
From soaring battlements,
Earth eyes Eternity.

Hugh MacDiarmid (1892–1978)

View in Strathtay. *From an engraving after Paul Sandby*

THE CARSE

It is a thousand sunsets since I lay
In many-birded Gowrie, and did know
Its shadow for my soul, that passionate Tay
Out of my heart did flow.

The immortal hour the hate of time defies.
Men of my loins a million years away
Shall have the gloom of Gowrie in their eyes,
And in their blood the Tay.

Lewis Spence (1874–1955)

SONNET

Slide soft faire Forth, and make a christall plaine,
Cut your white lockes, and on your foamie face
Let not a wrinckle bee, when you embrace
The boat that Earths Perfections doth containe.
Windes wonder, and through wondring holde your peace,
Or if that yee your hearts cannot restraine
From sending sighes, mov'd by a lovers case,
Sigh, and in her faire haire your selves enchaine:
Or take these sighes which absence makes arise
From mine oppressed brest and wave the sailes,
Or some sweet breath new brought from Paradise:
Flouds seeme to smile, love o'er the winds prevailes,
And yet hudge waves arise, the cause is this,
The ocean strives with Forth the boate to kisse.

William Drummond of Hawthornden (1585–1649)

'Queen Victoria and the Prince Consort at Hawthornden'. *William Allan*

Pittenweem. *Sam Bough*

WE'LL GO TO SEA NO MORE

Oh blythely shines the bonnie sun
    Upon the isle of May,
And blythely comes the morning tide
    Into St Andrew's Bay.
Then up, gude-man, the breeze is fair,
    And up, my braw bairns three;
There's gold in yonder bonnie boat
    That sails so well the sea!

I've seen the waves as blue as air,
    I've seen them green as grass;
But I never feared their heaving yet,
    From Grangemouth to the Bass.
I've seen the sea as black as pitch,
    I've seen it white as snow:
But I never feared its foaming yet,
    Though the winds blew high or low.

I never like the landsman's life,
    The earth is aye the same;
Give me the ocean for my dower,
    My vessel for my hame.
Give me the fields that no man ploughs,
    The farm that pays no fee:
Give me the bonny fish that dance
    Aye merrily in the sea!

The sun is up, and round Inchkeith
    The breezes softly blaw;
The gude-man has his lines aboard –
    Awa', my bairns, awa'.
An' ye'll be back by gloaming grey,
    An' bright the fire will low,
An' in your tales and songs we'll tell
    How weel the boat ye row.

Anonymous

KINNAIRD HEAD

I go North to cold, to home, to Kinnaird,
Fit monument for our time.
This is the outermost edge of Buchan.
Inland the sea birds range,
The tree's leaf has salt upon it,
The tree turns to the low stone wall.
And here a promontory rises towards Norway,
Irregular to the top of thin grey grass
Where the spindrift in storm lays its beads.
The water plugs in the cliff sides,
The gull cries from the clouds
This is the consummation of the plain.

O impregnable and very ancient rock,
Rejecting the violence of water,
Ignoring its accumulations and strategy,
You yield to history nothing.

George Bruce (1909–   )

HOMETOWN ELEGY

(for Aberdeen in Spring)

Glitter of mica at the windy corners,
Tar in the nostrils, under blue lamps budding
Like bubbles of glass and blue buds of a tree,
Night-shining shopfronts, or the sleek sun flooding
The broad abundant dying sprawl of the Dee:
For these and for their like my thoughts are mourners
That yet shall stand, though I come home no more,
Gas works, white ballroom, and the red brick baths
And salmon nets along a mile of shore,
Or beyond the municipal golf-course, the moorland paths
And the country lying quiet and full of farms.
This is the shape of a land that outlasts a strategy
And is not to be taken with rhetoric or arms.
Or my own room, with a dozen books on the bed
(Too late, still musing what I mused, I lie
And read too lovingly what I have read),
Brantôme, Spinoza, Yeats, the bawdy and wise,
Continuing their interminable debate,
With no conclusion, they conclude too late,
When their wisdom has fallen like a grey pall on my eyes.
Syne we maun part, there sall be nane remeid –
Unless my country is my pride, indeed,
Or I can make my town that homely fame
That Byron has, from boys in Carden Place,
Struggling home with books to midday dinner,
For whom he is not the romantic sinner,
The careless writer, the tormented face,
The hectoring bully or the noble fool,
But, just like Gordon or like Keith, a name:
A tall, proud statue at the Grammar School.

G. S. Fraser (1914–   )

'Brother and Sister'. *Joan Eardley*

CANEDOLIA

an off-concrete scotch fantasia

oa! hoy! awe! ba! mey!

who saw?
rhu saw rum. garve saw smoo. nigg saw tain. lairg saw lagg.
rigg saw cigg. largs saw haggs. tongue saw luss. mull saw yell.
stoer saw strone. drem saw muck. gask saw noss. unst saw cults.
echt saw banff. weem saw wick. trool saw twatt.

how far?
from largo to lunga from joppa to skibo from ratho to shona from
ulva to minto from tinto to tolsta from soutra to marsco from
braco to barra from alva to stobo from fogo to fada from gigha to
gogo from kelso to stroma from hirta to spango.

what is it like there?
och it' freuchie, it's faifley, it's wamphray, it's frandy, it's
sliddery.

what do you do?
we foindle and fungle, we bonkle and meigle and maxpoffle. we
scotstarvit, armit, wormit, and even whifflet. we play at crossstobs,
leuchars, gorbals, and finfan. we scavaig, and there's aye a bit of
tilquhilly. if it's wet, treshnish and mishnish.

what is the best of the country?
blinkbonny! airgold! thundergay!

and the worst?
scrishven, shiskine, scrabster, and snizort.

listen! what's that?
catacol and wauchope, never heed them.

tell us about last night
well, we had a wee ferintosh and we lay on the quiraing. it was
pure strontian!

but who was there?
petermoidart and craigenkenneth and cambusputtock and
ecclemuchty and corriehulish and balladolly and altnacanny and
clauchanvrechan and stronachlochan and auchenlachar and
tighnacrankie and tilliebruaich and killieharra and invervannach
and achnatudlem and machrishellach and inchtamurchan and
auchterfechan and kinlochculter and ardnawhallie and inver-
shuggle.

and what was the toast?
schiehallion! schiehallion! schiehallion!

Edwin Morgan (1920–   )

Acknowledgements

While the Editor and Publishers have done their best to trace the holders of copyright poems which have been included, they would be most grateful to be told of any that have proved impossible to trace.

The Editor would like to thank the following for permission to reproduce certain copyright poems:

W.H. Auden, *Night Mail* from THE ENGLISH AUDEN. Reprinted by permission of Faber and Faber Ltd.

Helen B. Cruickshank, *Ealasaid.* Reprinted by permission of Gordon Wright Publishing.

G. S. Fraser, *Hometown Elegy.* Reprinted by permission of the author.

Sir Alexander Gray, *Scotland.* Reprinted by permission of John Gray.

Norman MacCaig, *Musical Moment in Assynt* and *Sunset Ploughing* from THE WHITE BIRD. Reprinted by permission of Chatto and Windus.

Hugh MacDiarmid, *Montrose* and *Edinburgh* from COLLECTED POEMS. Reprinted by permission of Valda Grieve and Martin Brian and O'Keefe Ltd.

Edwin Morgan, *Canedolia.* Reprinted by permission of Edinburgh University Press.

Edwin Muir, *Childhood* from THE COLLECTED POEMS OF EDWIN MUIR. Reprinted by permission of Faber and Faber Ltd.

Robert Rendall, *Orkney Crofter.* Copyright of Mr R. P. Rendall.

Andrew Young, *The Cuillin Hills* from COMPLETE POEMS by Andrew Young, edited by Leonard Clark. Reprinted by permission of Martin Secker and Warburg Ltd.

Index of Authors

Index of Artists